YEAR 3

LANGUAGE CONVENTIONS

NAPLAN*-FORMAT PRACTICE TESTS
with answers

Essential preparation for Year 3
NAPLAN* Tests in Language Conventions

DON ROBENS

CORONEOS PUBLICATIONS

* These tests have been produced by Coroneos Publications independently of Australian governments and are not officially endorsed publications of the NAPLAN program

YEAR 3 LANGUAGE CONVENTIONS
NAPLAN*-FORMAT PRACTICE TESTS with answers
© Don Robens 2010
Published by Coroneos Publications 2010

ISBN 978-1-921565-43-4

* These tests have been produced by Coroneos Publications independently of Australian governments and are not officially endorsed publications of the NAPLAN program

THIS BOOK IS AVAILABLE FROM RECOGNISED BOOKSELLERS OR CONTACT:

Coroneos Publications
Telephone: (02) 9624 3977   Facsimile: (02) 9624 3717
Business Address: 6/195 Prospect Highway Seven Hills 2147
Postal Address: PO Box 2 Seven Hills 2147
Website: www. coroneos.com.au or www.basicskillsseries.com
E-mail: coroneospublications@westnet.com.au

Contents

NOTE:

• Students have 40 minutes to complete a test.

• Students must use 2B or HB pencils only.

Read the text *Kangaroo*.
The spelling mistakes have been underlined.
Write the correct spelling for each word on the line provided.

Kangaroo

Here is a kangaroo.

It has a long <u>tale</u>.   1 _____

Some have <u>gray</u> fur.   2 _____

Kangaroos have long <u>eers</u>.   3 _____

The spelling mistakes in these sentences have been underlined.
Write the correct spelling for each underlined word on the line provided.

4   The dog was hungry <u>afer</u> not eating all day. 4 _____

5   My dad <u>gos</u> to work every morning.   5 _____

6   The day went <u>quikly</u>.   6 _____

7   The moon was seen in the night <u>ski</u>.   7 _____

The spelling mistakes in these sentences have been underlined. Write the correct spelling for each underlined word on the line provided.

8 The book was on the <u>tabel</u>.   8 _____

9 On the beach were <u>meny</u> interesting shells. 9 _____

10 Do you like this <u>colore</u>?   10 _____

11 Over <u>ther</u> is the sea.   11 _____

12 The <u>raine</u> was filling the water tank.   12 _____

**The words below are pairs of opposites.
In each pair, one of the words is spelled incorrectly.
Write the correct spelling of the word on the line provided.**

Opposites

high   lowe   13 _____

tall   shorte   14 _____

bigger   smaler   15 _____

Each sentence has one word that is incorrect.
Write the correct spelling of the word on the line provided.

16 He was a happie baby.   16 _____

17 Sue was riting a letter to send in the mail.   17 _____

18 Jack jumped over the skiping rope.   18 _____

19 A docter put a bandage on my arm.   19 _____

20 The shool was open early.   20 _____

21 I was leerning to read faster.   21 _____

22 My mothar made my lunch for me.   22 _____

23 The bookshop was in the shoping centre. 23 _____

Read the text Colours. The text has some gaps.
Choose the correct word to fill each gap.

Colours

Shade one
bubble

The artist used many colours when he was   24   .

He   25   these colours to paint.

His work   26   very popular.

---

24   painting   painteing   paints
              ○   ○   ○

---

25   used   use   used to
              ○   ○   ○

---

26   were   was   written
              ○   ○   ○

---

27 Which word correctly completes the sentence?

Kim ⬜ the birds building the nest.

watch   watching   watched
○   ○   ○

28 Which word or words correctly complete the sentence

Have you ⬜ the new bridge?

saw   seen   sawn   see
○   ○   ○   ○

Which word correctly completes the sentences?

29 The class listened carefully ⬜ the story.

too   two   to
○   ○   ○

30 The car was driven along the ⬜.

rode   road   roade
○   ○   ○

Read the text Books. The text has some gaps.
Choose the correct word or words to fill each gap.

Books

The large book was ▮31▮ the teacher's desk.

▮32▮ a wonderful book.

▮33▮ teacher read us a story from it each day.

31	up	on	to
	○	○	○

32	It's	It	Its
	○	○	○

33	our	Oh	Our
	○	○	○

34 Which word correctly completes the sentence?

Shade one bubble

It was an ▮▮▮ dog.

sad	good	angry	dangerous
○	○	○	○

Read the sentences about _Bubbles_. They have some gaps. Choose the correct word to fill each gap.

Bubbles

The children **35** bubbles.

The bubbles **36** up into the air.

They floated across the garden **37**

38 loved blowing bubbles.

35

blue	blow	blew
○	○	○

36

rise	rose	risen
○	○	○

37

?	.	,
○	○	○

38

everywon	everyone	Everyone
○	○	○

**Read the text Zoo Visit. The text has some gaps.
Choose the correct word or words to fill each gap.**

Zoo Visit

Shade one bubble

My family [39] the zoo.

We saw [40] and koalas.

We were [41] at the end of the day.

We [42] the bus home after leaving the zoo.

---

39   visit   visited   visiting
              ○   ○   ○

---

40 ○ apes, elephants, snakes

    ○ apes, elephants and snakes

    ○ apes elephants and snakes

---

41   tired   tyred   tire
              ○   ○   ○

---

42   catch   caught   catched
              ○   ○   ○

Shade one bubble

43 Which answer correctly completes the sentence?

The girl wrote the story ______ checked her work.

○ so ○ and then ○ because ○ when

44 Which answer correctly completes the sentence?

"I like bananas ______ than oranges," said Jo.

○ best ○ better ○ more better

45 Which word correctly completes the sentence?

The fish swam ______ the still water.

○ threw ○ through ○ throw

46 Which sentence is correct?

- ○ My mother and I read the book.
- ○ My mother and me read the book.
- ○ Me and my mother read the book.
- ○ I and my mother read the book.

Test 1   **Answers**

1. tail   **2.** grey   **3.** ears   **4.** after   **5.** goes   **6.** quickly   **7.** sky

8. table   **9.** many   **10.** colour   **11.** there   **12.** rain   **13.** low   **14.** shorter

15. smaller   **16.** happy   **17.** writing   **18.** skipping   **19.** doctor   **20.** school

21. learning   **22.** mother   **23.** shopping   **24.** painting   **25.** used   **26.** was

27. watched   **28.** seen   **29.** to   **30.** road   **31.** on   **32.** It's   **33.** Our

34. angry   **35.** blew   **36.** rose   **37.** .(full stop)   **38.** Everyone   **39.** visited

40. apes, elephants, snakes   **41.** tired   **42.** caught   **43.** and then

44. better   **45.** through   **46.** My mother and I read the book.

Read the text *Shops*.
The spelling mistakes have been underlined.
Write the correct spelling for each word on the line.

Shops

Here is a shopping trolley.

It has a <u>specal</u> frame

1. _____

It can carry <u>meny</u> things.

2. _____

It is in a <u>besy</u> place.

3. _____

The spelling mistakes in these sentences have been underlined.
Write the correct spelling for each underlined word on the line
provided.

4 The man was <u>hungree</u> by lunch time.   4 _____

5 My mum goes to work every <u>mornin</u>.   5 _____

6 The library was <u>quite</u>.   6 _____

7 The bat flew during the <u>nite</u>.   7 _____

The spelling mistakes in these sentences have been underlined. Write the correct spelling for each underlined word on the line provided.

8 The childrun read well.   8 _____

9 On the shelves were many intresting books. 9 _____

10 Did you by the book yet?   10 _____

11 Over their is a cave.   11 _____

12 We no the answer.   12 _____

**The words below are pairs of opposites.
In each pair, one of the words is spelled incorrectly.
Write the correct spelling of the word on the line provided.**

Opposites

big	littel	13 _____
today	tomorow	14 _____
plus	minuss	15 _____

Each sentence has one word that is incorrect.
Write the correct spelling of the word on the line provided.

16 The wether was sunny.   16 _____

17 It was a suprise.   17 _____

18 She aet the apple.   18 _____

19 The dog was in the animal hospittal.   19 _____

20 The libary was busy.   20 _____

21 The windowes were open.   21 _____

22 The lengh of the snake was surprising.   22 _____

23 At the zoo were many animels.   23 _____

**Read the text *Cars*. The text has some gaps.
Choose the correct word to fill each gap.**

Cars

Shade one bubble

The cars were in the ⬛24 .

They ⬛25 all sparkling.

⬛26 you seen garages like this?

---

24   garagge   garage   Garage

⚬   ⚬   ⚬

---

25   were   was   where

⚬   ⚬   ⚬

---

26   has   have   Have

⚬   ⚬   ⚬

27 **Which answer correctly completes the sentence?**

[   ] the doctor give you any medicine?.

Don't   Do   Did

○   ○   ○

28 **Which word correctly completes the sentence?**

The driver [   ] carefully.

drive   drove   Drove   driven

○   ○   ○   ○

Which word correctly completes the sentences?

29 [   ] books were on the table.

Too   Two   To

○   ○   ○

30 The children [   ] in the playground.

were   where   was

○   ○   ○

Read the text *Eagles*. The text has some gaps.
Choose the correct word or words to fill each gap.

Eagles

Shade one bubble

The eagle is a ⬛31 bird.

⬛32 you seen one?

How fast can it fly ⬛33

---

31   larg   large   larrge
             ○   ○   ○

---

32   have   Has   Have
             ○   ○   ○

---

33   ?   .   ,
             ○   ○   ○

---

34 **Which word correctly completes the sentence?**

It was an ▮▮▮▮ ant.

big	small	unusual	black
○	○	○	○

Read the text *Balloons*. The text has some gaps.
Choose the correct word to fill each gap.

Balloons

Balloons **35** full of air.

They can float **36** the air.

Balloons can be many **37** .

38 that shop sell balloons?

---

35   is   are   have
             ○   ○   ○

---

36   through   though   threw
             ○   ○   ○

---

37   colors   coloures   colours
             ○   ○   ○

---

38   Do   Does   Don't
             ○   ○   ○

Read the text Ships. The text has some gaps.
Choose the correct word or words to fill each gap.

Ships

Shade one bubble

Several ships ▮39▮ in the harbour.

We saw ▮40▮ and other ships.

▮41▮ you notice them?

Ships are ▮42▮ important form of transport.

---

39 was ○   were ○   where ○

---

40 ○ large, small.

○ large small.

○ largest, little.

---

41 did ○   Did ○   Don't ○

---

42 an ○   a ○   am ○

43 **Which answer correctly completes the sentence?**

Shade one bubble

The swimmer swam in the pool ▮▮▮ left it.

so   and then   because   when

○   ○   ○   ○

44 **Which word correctly completes the sentence?**

"I write ▮▮▮ than I draw," said Mary.

best   better   more better

○   ○   ○

45 **Which word correctly completes the sentence?**

He ▮▮▮ the horse.

draw   drew   drawn

○   ○   ○

46 **Which sentence is correct?**

○ My brother and me helped.

○ My brother and I helped.

○ Me and my brother helped.

○ I and my brother helped.

Test 2 **Answers**

1. special   **2.** many   **3.** busy   **4.** hungry   **5.** morning   **6.** quiet   **7.** night

8. children   **9.** interesting   **10.** buy **11.** there   **12.** know   **13.** little

14. tomorrow   **15.** minus   **16.** weather   **17.** surprise   **18.** ate

19. hospital   **20.** library   **21.** windows   **22.** length   **23.** animals

24. garage   **25.** were   **26.** Have   **27.** Did   **28.** drove   **29.** Two

30. were   **31.** large   **32.** Have   **33.** ?   **34.** unusual   **35.** are

36. through   **37.** colours   **38.** Does   **39.** were   **40.** large, small

41. Did   **42.** an   **43.** and then   **44.** better   **45.** drew

46. My brother and I helped.

Read the text *Television*.
The spelling mistakes have been underlined.
Write the correct spelling for each word on the line.

Television

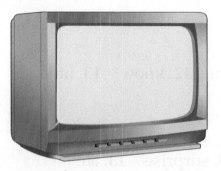

The television is in a shop.

It is for <u>sail</u>.   **1** _____

It costs a lot of <u>mony</u>.   **2** _____

It has a flat <u>scren</u>.   **3** _____

The spelling mistakes in these sentences have been underlined.
Write the correct spelling for each underlined word on the line provided.

4. The desk was one <u>meter</u> long.   **4** _____

5   They worked for one <u>houw</u>.   **5** _____

6   It was eleven <u>oclock</u>.   **6** _____

7   The <u>yeer</u> was a busy one.   **7** _____

The spelling mistakes in these sentences have been underlined. Write the correct spelling for each underlined word on the line provided.

8   They were good <u>frends</u>.

8 _____

9   They were <u>swiming</u>.

9 _____

10 <u>Dose</u> the dog often bark?

10 _____

11 On <u>Tuseday</u> we saw the insect.

11 _____

12 We knew the <u>anser</u>.

12 _____

**The words below are pairs of opposites.
In each pair, one of the words is spelled incorrectly.
Write the correct spelling of the word on the line provided.**

Opposites

right	letf	13 _____
strong	week	14 _____
last	fist	15 _____

Each sentence has one word that is incorrect.
Write the correct spelling of the word on the line provided.

16 The writeing was neat.

16 _____

17 It was Wedesday.

17 _____

18 The hare cut was finished.

18 _____

19 There were fore books to read.

19 _____

20 The miror was shiny.

20 _____

21 The sun was shinning.

21 _____

22 Unckle Tom rang.

22 _____

23 Arnty Ruth also rang.

23 _____

Read the text Books. The text has some gaps.
Choose the correct word to fill each gap.

Books

Shade one bubble

The books were ⬛ 24 .

⬛ 25 that one a good one?

⬛ 26 bought one of them.

---

24   colorful   colourfull   colourful

         ◯   ◯   ◯

---

25   ISnt   Isn't   isn't

         ◯   ◯   ◯

---

26   john   JOHN   John

         ◯   ◯   ◯

27 **Which word correctly completes the sentence?**

[ ] the mail arrived?

has   Has   Haven't

◯   ◯   ◯

28 Which word correctly completes the sentence?

The friend waved [ ] .

goodbuy   goodbye   goodby

◯   ◯   ◯

Which word correctly completes the sentences?

29 The dog went [ ] .

too   two   to

◯   ◯   ◯

30 The children went [ ] the classroom.

to   too   two

◯   ◯   ◯

Read the text *Water*. The text has some gaps.
Choose the correct word or words to fill each gap.

Water

Shade one bubble

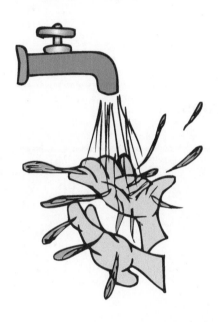

Water covers most **31** the earth.

32 talked about water.

Water is a liquid **33** cools and cleans.

---

31   off   of   for

              ◯   ◯   ◯

---

32   Mum   mum

              ◯   ◯

---

33   ?   ,   .

              ◯   ◯   ◯

34 Which word correctly completes the sentence?

It was an ▮▮▮ story.

great	interesting	happy	long
○	○	○	○

Read the text *Paper*. The text has some gaps.
Choose the correct word to fill each gap.

Paper

Paper **35** from trees.

36 was paper on the shelf.

Do you need paper now **37**

Do you **38** how paper is made

---

35   comes   come   are coming

         ○   ○   ○

---

36   Their   There   They're

         ○   ○   ○

---

37   .   ,   ?

         ○   ○   ○

---

38   no   know   knew

         ○   ○   ○

© Don Robens
Coroneos Publications

Year 3 Language Conventions
NAPLAN*-Format Practice Tests

Read the text *Science*. The text has some gaps.
Choose the correct word or words to fill each gap.

Science

Shade one
bubble

We are ▮39▮ a lot about science.

▮40▮ and stars are Science topics.

Plants and animals ▮41▮ also Science topics.

You can ▮42▮ much by studying science.

---

39   learn   taughted   learning
                ○   ○   ○

---

40   ○ air, water, space
         ○ air water space
         ○ Air, water, space

---

41   is   are   aren't
                ○   ○   ○

---

42   taught   learn   learnt
                ○   ○   ○

Shade one bubble

43 **Which word can be used instead of the underlined words?**

I am going to the library. I like it <u>in the library</u>.

here   there   where   when

○   ○   ○   ○

44 **Which word correctly completes the sentence?**

"That is the better ▭ of the two," said Roger.

by   bye   buy

○   ○   ○

45 **Which word correctly completes the sentence?**

Which is the best book you ▭ read?

has   have   half

○   ○   ○

46 **Which sentence is correct?**

○ James, jill and Jo worked together.

○ James, jill and jo worked together.

○ James Jill and Jo worked together.

○ James, Jill and Jo worked together.

Test 3   **Answers**

1. sale   **2.** money   **3.** screen   **4.** metre   **5.** hour   **6.** o'clock   **7.** year

8. friends **9.** swimming **10.** Does **11.** Tuesday **12.** answer **13.** left **14.** weak

15. first   **16.** writing   **17.** Wednesday   **18.** hair   **19.** four   **20.** mirror

21. shining   **22.** Uncle   **23.** Aunty   **24.** colourful   **25.** Isn't   **26.** John

27. Has   **28.** goodbye   **29.** too   **30.** to   **31.** of   **32.** Mum   **33.** , (comma)

34. interesting   **35.** comes   **36.** There   **37.** ? (question)   **38.** know

39. learning   **40.** Air, water, space   **41.** are   **42.** learn   **43.** there

44. buy   **45.** have   **46.** James, Jill and Jo worked together.

Read the text *Numbers*.
The spelling mistakes have been underlined.
Write the correct spelling for each word on the line.

Numbers

Numbers are useful.

One, two, <u>there</u>...   1. _____

One <u>hunded</u>...   2. _____

One <u>thosand</u>...   3. _____

The spelling mistakes in these sentences have been underlined.
Write the correct spelling for each underlined word on the line
provided.

4 There were <u>eaght</u> eggs.   4 _____

5 <u>Halfe</u> the eggs were cooked.   5 _____

6 <u>Fore</u> eggs were left.   6 _____

7 They cost three <u>dollers</u>.   7 _____

The spelling mistakes in these sentences have been underlined. Write the correct spelling for each underlined word on the line provided.

8 The room was <u>cleen</u>.

8 _____

9 Everyone was <u>happey</u>.

9 _____

10 The engine was <u>noisey</u>.

10 _____

11 On <u>Saterday</u> we read a book.

11 _____

12 The answer was <u>rong</u>.

12 _____

The words below are pairs of opposites. In each pair, one of the words is spelled incorrectly. Write the correct spelling of the word on the line provided.

Opposites

table	chaire	13. _____
pen	pensil	14. _____
student	teecher	15. _____

**Each sentence has one word that is incorrect.
Write the correct spelling of the word on the line provided.**

16 We could hear musik.   16. _____

17 Trees shaded the playgrond.   17. _____

18 Along the beech were shells.   18. _____

19 We built a sandcastel.   19. _____

20 The oceen was huge.   20. _____

21 There were no cloudes in the sky.   21. _____

22 The tap was driping.   22. _____

23 A whisstle blew.   23. _____

Read the text *Sounds*. The text has some gaps.
Choose the correct word to fill each gap.

Sounds

Shade one bubble

The wind was 24 .

" 25   do that!" yelled Dad.

26 was very happy.

---

24   houling   howling   Howling
         ⬭   ⬭   ⬭

---

25   Don't   Dont   don't
         ⬭   ⬭   ⬭

---

26   sally   Sally   SALLY
         ⬭   ⬭   ⬭

27 **Which word correctly completes the sentence?**

Where ▮▮ the book?

Shade one bubble

were	have	is
○	○	○

28 **Which word correctly completes the sentence?**

The train stopped ▮▮ people could safely leave and enter it.

were	wear	where
○	○	○

Which word correctly completes the sentences?

29 The man ▮▮ to carry the heavy table.

tryed	tried	try
○	○	○

30 It was ▮▮ beautiful day.

a	am	an
○	○	○

Read the text *Tastes*. The text has some gaps.
Choose the correct word or words to fill each gap.

Tastes

Shade one bubble

Honey **31** sweet.

32 is salty.

Taste buds taste sweet **33** sour and salty things.

---

31   is   are   am
           ○   ○   ○

---

32   salt   Salt
           ○   ○   ○

---

33   ,   ?   .
           ○   ○   ○

34 Which word correctly completes the sentence?

Shade one bubble

It was an ▭ day.

    sunny   rainy   overcast   cloudy

    ◯   ◯   ◯   ◯

**Read the text Time. The text has some gaps.
Choose the correct word to fill each gap.**

Time

35 is the first month of the year.

36 twelve months in a year.

Wow **37** Time is going quickly.

The **38** year is passing quickly!

---

35   january   Janary   January

        ◯   ◯   ◯

---

36   They're   There's   There're

        ◯   ◯   ◯

---

37   .   !   ?

        ◯   ◯   ◯

---

38   hole   whole   hold

        ◯   ◯   ◯

Read the text *Months*. The text has some gaps.
Choose the correct word or words to fill each gap.

Months

How many months are there `39`

`40` are the autumn months.

`41` is the abbreviation for December.

"Happy birthday `42` " cheered the friends.

---

39   .   ?   ,
                    ○   ○   ○

---

40 ○ march, april and may
     ○ March, April and May
     ○ March April and May

---

41   dec.   dec   Dec.
                ○   ○   ○

---

42   .   !   ?
                    ○   ○   ○

43 Which word can be used instead of the underlined words?

I am going to the museum. I like it <u>in the museum</u>.

their   they're   there   then
○   ○   ○   ○

44 Which word correctly completes the sentence?

The truck ▮▮▮ the car.

pass   past   passed
○   ○   ○

45 Which word correctly completes the sentence?

Which is the ▮▮▮ book you have ever read?

best   better   bestest
○   ○   ○

46 Which sentence is correct?

○ "Have you finished?" asked Tom.

○ Have you finished? asked Tom.

○ "have you finished?" asked Tom.

○ "Have you finished" asked Tom.

Test 4   **Answers**

1. three   **2.** hundred   **3.** thousand   **4.** eight   **5.** Half   **6.** Four   **7.** dollars

8. clean   **9.** happy   **10.** noisy   **11.** Saturday   **12.** wrong   **13.** chair

14. pencil   **15.** teacher   **16.** music   **17.** playground **18.** beach

19. sandcastle   **20.** ocean   **21.** clouds   **22.** dripping   **23.** whistle

24. howling   **25.** Don't   **26.** Sally   **27.** is   **28.** where   **29.** tried   **30.** a

31. is   **32.** Salt   **33.** , (comma)   **34.** overcast   **35.** January   **36.** There're

37. ! (exclamation)   **38.** whole   **39.** ? (question)

40. March, April and May are the autumn months.   **41.** Dec.

42. ! (exclamation)   **43.** there   **44.** passed   **45.** best   **46.** "Have you finished?" asked Tom.

Read the text *Time*. The spelling mistakes have been underlined. Write the correct spelling for each word on the line.

Time

Time is measuring.

There are <u>sekonds</u>.

1 _____

There are <u>minites</u>.

2 _____

There are <u>houres</u>.

3 _____

The spelling mistakes in these sentences have been underlined. Write the correct spelling for each underlined word on the line provided.

4 It was a special <u>holliday</u>.

4 _____

5 We read <u>dayly</u>.

5 _____

6 The ants were <u>leeving</u> the nest.

6 _____

7 Buses <u>arived</u> early.

7 _____

The spelling mistakes in these sentences have been underlined. Write the correct spelling for each underlined word on the line provided.

8 The flag was <u>riseing</u>.   8 _____

9 The teacher was <u>speeking</u> quietly.   9 _____

10 <u>Remeber</u> your lunch.   10

11 The door was <u>closeing</u>.   11

12 We could <u>here</u> the bee flying.   12

**The words below are pairs of opposites.
In each pair, one of the words is spelled incorrectly.
Write the correct spelling of the word on the line provided.**

Opposites

standing   siting   13. _____

buses   traines   14. _____

cars   bicyles   15. _____

**Each sentence has one word that is incorrect.
Write the correct spelling of the word on the line provided.**

16 The waves were calmn.   16 _____

17 The weether was fine.   17 _____

18 It was just the begining.   18 _____

19 That's the middal of the page.   19 _____

20 We tryed to do well.   20 _____

21 I heerd the noise.   21 _____

22 We wattched the game.   22 _____

23 Jessica cleened her room.   23 _____

Read the text *Homes*. The text has some gaps.
Choose the correct word to fill each gap.

Homes

Shade one bubble

On top of the home is a 24 .

25. "I 25 do it!" cried Tim.

26 was a good friend.

24	roof	roofe	rooft
	○	○	○

25	cant	can't	Can't
	○	○	○

26	Pipi	pipi	PIPPI
	○	○	○

27 Which word correctly completes the sentence?

Where 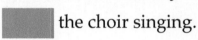 the coin roll?

Did	don't	did
◯	◯	◯

28 Which word correctly completes the sentence?

▮ the choir singing.

Here	Hear	hear
◯	◯	◯

Which word correctly completes the sentences?

29 He ▮ the ball well.

threw	through	throw

30 I bought a ▮ of fruit.

peace	piece	peice
◯	◯	◯

Read the text *Weights*. The text has some gaps. Choose the correct word or words to fill each gap.

Weights

Shade one bubble

The elephant was ▨**31** .

▨**32** carefully watching the elephant.

"It is really heavy ▨**33** " gasped Kim.

---

31   heevy   heavy   heavi
            ◯   ◯   ◯

---

32   we're   We're   Where
            ◯   ◯   ◯

---

33   ,   ?   !
            ◯   ◯   ◯

---

34 **Which word correctly completes the sentence?**

Shade one bubble

The car was an ▨ car.

blue	cheap	expensive	model
○	○	○	○

Read the text *People*. The text has some gaps.
Choose the correct word to fill each gap.

People

They are our 35 .

36 a lovely person.

The whole family was 37 .

38 cousins lived a long way away.

35

neeghbours	neighbours	neighbors
○	○	○

36

She's	Shes	she's
○	○	○

37

their	there	they're
○	○	○

38

Jacks	Jacks'	Jack's
○	○	○

**Read the text *Trees*. The text has some gaps.
Choose the correct word or words to fill each gap.**

Trees

Shade one bubble

The tree had many 39 .

40 and leaves.

Rows of fruit trees 41 near the river.

"Can you help me 42 " asked the little girl.

---

39   leafs   leafes   leaves
             ○   ○   ○

---

40 ○ A tree has roots, a trunk

       ○ A tree have roots a trunk

       ○ a tree have roots, a trunk

---

41   grew   grue   are grewing
             ○   ○   ○

---

42   .   !   ?
             ○   ○   ○

43 Which word can be used instead of the underlined words?

Shade one bubble

<u>At this point of time</u> we will read quietly.

now	Once	Now	next
○	○	○	

44 Which word correctly completes the sentence?

Each student ▉ working quietly.

are	is	were
○	○	○

45 Which word correctly completes the sentence?

Which is the ▉ way to go – to the right or to the left?

safe	safer	safest
○	○	○

46 Which sentence is correct?

○ Sam asked, "Did you like that story."

○ Sam asked "Did you like that story?"

○ Sam asked, "Did you like that story?"

○ Sam asked, Did you like that story?"

Test 5 **Answers**

1. seconds **2.** minutes **3.** hours **4.** holiday **5.** daily **6.** leaving

7. arrived **8.** rising **9.** speaking **10.** Remember **11.** closing **12.** hear

13. sitting **14.** trains **15.** bicycles **16.** calm **17.** weather **18.** beginning

19. middle **20.** tried **21.** heard **22.** watched **23.** cleaned **24.** roof

25. can't **26.** Pipi **27.** did **28.** Hear **29.** threw **30.** piece **31.** heavy

32. We're **33.** ! **34.** expensive **35.** neighbours **36.** She's **37.** there

38. Jack's **39.** leaves **40.** A tree has roots, a trunk and leaves.

41. grew **42.** ? (question) **43.** Now **44.** is

45. safer **46.** Sam asked, "Did you like that story?"

Read the text *Reading*.
The spelling mistakes have been underlined.
Write the correct spelling for each word on the line.

Reading

Reading is fun.

There are <u>storyes</u> to read.   **1** _____

There are <u>pickures</u> to see.   **2** _____

There are <u>witers</u> to know about.   **3** _____

The spelling mistakes in these sentences have been underlined.
Write the correct spelling for each underlined word on the line
provided.

4 The <u>awthor</u> wrote the book.   **4** _____

5 The bus was <u>traveling</u> quickly.   **5** _____

6 The car was driven <u>carefuly</u>.   **6** _____

7 The <u>breaks</u> were used to stop the car.   **7** _____

The spelling mistakes in these sentences have been underlined. Write the correct spelling for each underlined word on the line provided.

8 That is the <u>center</u> of the circle.

8 _____

9 The <u>biulding</u> was a tall one.

9 _____

10 <u>Busses</u> moved along the road.

10 _____

11 The <u>streat</u> was busy.

11 _____

12 They lived in a city <u>suburd</u>.

12 _____

The words below are pairs of opposites. In each pair, one of the words is spelled incorrectly. Write the correct spelling of the word on the line provided.

Opposites

today	yesturday	13 _____
answers	qestions	14 _____
easy	dificult	15 _____

Each sentence has one word that is incorrect.
Write the correct spelling of the word on the line provided.

16 The sissors were used carefully.   16 _____

17 The line was straght.   17 _____

18 It was a good speach.   18 _____

19 That's the correct adress.   19 _____

20 We checked our cloths.   20 _____

21 That was my favorite colour.   21 _____

22 Is this usefull?   22 _____

23 We watched the teems play.   23 _____

Read the text *Gardens*. The text has some gaps.
Choose the correct word to fill each gap.

Gardens

Shade one bubble

The garden ▣24 was rich.

"I ▣25 do it!" cried Kath.

▣26 beautiful!" said Jill.

---

24   soile   siol   soil
             ⬭   ⬭   ⬭

---

25   didn't   didnot   didnt
             ⬭   ⬭   ⬭

---

26   Thats   thats   That's
             ⬭   ⬭   ⬭

27 Which word correctly completes the sentence?

◻ did the dog go?

Were   Where   Wear
○   ○   ○

28 Which word correctly completes the sentence?

We ◻ the shoes from the shop.

brought   bought   bort
○   ○   ○

Which word correctly completes the sentences?

29 They ◻ where the school was located.

new   known   knew
○   ○   ○

30 I looked at the ◻ .

photos   photoes   fotos
○   ○   ○

Read the text *Houses*. The text has some gaps.
Choose the correct word or words to fill each gap.

Houses

Shade one bubble

The windows were made of 31 .

 32   many houses in the street.

"Is it heavy 33 " questioned Kim.

---

31   glas   glase   glass

          ○   ○   ○

---

32   They're   There're   There

          ○   ○   ○

---

33   ,   ?   !

          ○   ○   ○

34 Which word correctly completes the sentence?

Over the fence flew an ▨ bird.

big	small	attractive	little
○	○	○	○

Read the text *Schools*. The text has some gaps.
Choose the correct word to fill each gap.

Schools

The rooms had **35** in them.

36 a clever student.

That is **37** home.

This is **38** bicycle.

35	cupbords	cupboards	cupboardes'
	○	○	○

36	He's	he's	Hes
	○	○	○

37	their	there	thear
	○	○	○

38	Dads	Dad's	Dads'
	○	○	○

**Read the text *Maths*. The text has some gaps.
Choose the correct word or words to fill each gap.**

Maths

Shade one bubble

In Maths we use **39** .

40 and multiply.

That is the second question **41** finished.

"What do I do next **42** " asked George.

---

39   numberes   numbers   numbars
         ○   ○   ○

---

40   ○ We learnt to add, subtract

   ○ We learnt to add subtract

   ○ we learnt to add, subtract

---

41   Ive   Iv'e   I've
         ○   ○   ○

---

42   ,   !   ?
         ○   ○   ○

43 **Which word should not be used in this sentence?**

They have got a beautiful garden.

have	got	a	garden
◯	◯	◯	◯

---

44 **Which word correctly completes the sentence?**

All students ▮ very busy.

was	is	were
◯	◯	◯

---

45 **Which word correctly completes the sentence?**

It was the ▮ story we had ever heard.

happy	happier	happiest
◯	◯	◯

---

46 **Which sentence is correct?**

◯ The doctor inquired, "Did you hear that.

◯ The doctor inquired "Did you hear that."

◯ The doctor inquired, "Did you hear that?"

◯ The doctor inquired, "Did you hear that."

Test 6   **Answers**

1. stories   2. pictures   3. writers 4. author   5. travelling   6. carefully

7. brakes   8. centre   9. building   10. Buses   11. street   12. suburb

13. yesterday   14. questions   15. difficult   16. scissors   17. straight

18. speech   19. address   20. clothes   21. favourite   22. useful

23. teams   24. soil   25. didn't   26. That's   27. Where   28. bought

29. knew   30. photos   31. glass   32. There're   33. ?   34. attractive

35. cupboards   36. He's   37. their   38. Dad's   39. numbers

40. We learnt to add, subtract and multiply.   41. I've   42. ? (question)

43. got   44. were   45. happiest   46. The doctor inquired, "Did you hear that?"

Read the text *Clothes*.
The spelling mistakes have been underlined.
Write the correct spelling for each word on the line.

Clothes

Clothes are useful.

There are many <u>colors</u> to see.   1 _____

There are many <u>paterns</u> to see.   2 _____

Clothes may be <u>woolen</u>, cotton…   3 _____

The spelling mistakes in these sentences have been underlined.
Write the correct spelling for each underlined word on the line
provided.

4 They were <u>exersising</u>.   4 _____

_____

5 The people were <u>liffting</u> the furniture.   5 _____

_____

6 Some were <u>katching</u> a ball.   6 _____

_____

7 Some were <u>bounsing</u> a ball.   7 _____

The spelling mistakes in these sentences have been underlined. Write the correct spelling for each underlined word on the line provided.

8 That is the railway <u>stathon</u>.   8 _____

9 The <u>camerra</u> was a modern one.   9 _____

10 The <u>scissers</u> were sharp.   10 _____

11 The people sat <u>togethar</u>.   11 _____

12 The tree fell <u>aganst</u> the house.   12 _____

The words below are pairs of opposites. In each pair, one of the words is spelled incorrectly. Write the correct spelling of the word on the line provided.

Opposites

noisy	quite	13 _____
reader	writter	14 _____
war	pease	15 _____

Each sentence has one word that is incorrect.
Write the correct spelling of the word on the line provided.

16 The sientists were busy.   16 _____

17 The train driver saw the signel.   17 _____

18 It was a good idee.   18 _____

19 That's the bigest ocean.   19 _____

20 We drew a squaire.   20 _____

21 That is a coutry home.   21 _____

22 Is this pear of shoes clean?   22 _____

23 We climbed the mountaine.   23 _____

**Read the text *Time*. The text has some gaps.
Choose the correct word to fill each gap.**

Time

Shade one bubble

Each **24** went quickly.

" **25** do it!" said James.

"You **26** much time left," said Mum.

---

24   month   moonth   monthe
           ○   ○   ○

---

25   Isn't   I'll   I've
           ○   ○   ○

---

26   don't   haven't   won't
           ○   ○   ○

27 Which word correctly completes the sentence?

"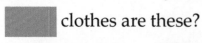 the dog?" asked Mrs Smith.

   Were's   Where's   Wears

    ◯   ◯   ◯

28. Which word correctly completes the sentence?

      clothes are these?

  Whose   Who's   Whos'

   ◯   ◯   ◯

Which word correctly completes the sentences?

29 Is this   ?

  yours   your's   yores

  ◯   ◯   ◯

30 They ate the   pizza.

  hole   whole

  ◯   ◯

Read the text *Colours*. The text has some gaps.
Choose the correct word or words to fill each gap.

Colours

Shade one bubble

The colours were [31] .

[32] see many colours.

"Is that real [33] " asked Bob.

---

31   beatiful   beautiful   beautifull
          ⬭   ⬭   ⬭

---

32   You'll   Youll   You'l
          ⬭   ⬭   ⬭

---

33   ,   ?   !
          ⬭   ⬭   ⬭

---

34 **Which word correctly completes the sentence?**

Shade one bubble

It is a ▮ school.

interesting	enormous	attractive	wonderful
○	○	○	○

Read the text *Fruit*. The text has some gaps.
Choose the correct word to fill each gap.

Fruit

The **35** were tasty.

36 many apples were on the table.

37 fruit trees were healthy.

38 lunch included a piece of fruit.

35	bananas	bannanas	bananes
	○	○	○

36	To	Two	Too
	○	○	○

37	their	There	Their
	○	○	○

38	Annes	Annes'	Anne's
	○	○	○

Read the text _Sounds_. The text has some gaps.
Choose the correct word or words to fill each gap.

Sounds

Shade one
bubble

The insect's 39 was quiet.

40 and squeaks.

They 41 finished yet.

"What an unusual sound 42 " exclaimed George.

---

39   buzz   buz   buzzes
            ○   ○   ○

---

40 ○ we heard creaks, drips
        ○ We heard creaks drips
        ○ We heard creaks, drips

---

41   havent   haven't   havenot
            ○   ○   ○

---

42   ,   !   ?
            ○   ○   ○

43 **Which word should not be used in this sentence?**

That is a more beautiful flower.

That	is	more	beautiful
○	○	○	○

44 **Which word correctly completes the sentence?**

All bees _____ very busy in the hive.

are	is	was
○	○	○

45 **Which word correctly completes the sentence?**

That must be the _____ street in the whole city.

busy	busier	busiest
○	○	○

46 **Which sentence is correct?**

○ "Did you hear that?" questioned Liz.

○ "Did you hear that," questioned Liz.

○ "Did you hear that." questioned Liz.

○ "Did you hear that!" questioned Liz.

Test 7 **Answers**

1. colours   **2.** patterns   **3.** woollen   **4.** exercising   **5.** lifting   **6.** catching

7. bouncing   **8.** station   **9.** camera   **10.** scissors   **11.** together

12. against   **13.** quiet   **14.** writer   **15.** peace   **16.** scientists   **17.** signal

18. idea   **19.** biggest   **20.** square   **21.** country   **22.** pair   **23.** mountain

24. month   **25.** I'll   **26.** haven't   **27.** Where's   **28.** Whose   **29.** yours

30. whole   **31.** beautiful   **32.** You'll   **33.** ?   **34.** wonderful

35. bananas   **36.** Too   **37.** Their   **38.** Anne's   **39.** buzz

40. We heard creaks, drips and squeaks. **41.** haven't   **42.** ! (exclamation)

43. more   **44.** are   **45.** busiest   **46.** "Did you hear that?" questioned Liz.